DIARYSOULS

A MIRROR TO YOUR SOUL

TEAM DIARYSOULS

Contents

Contents

Foreword

Kangkana Chakravarty

I was delighted when Diary Souls asked me to write a foreword for their new book, I mean who wouldn't love to appreciate the unique approach that Diary Souls have come out with; my interaction with this wonderful team was like a fortunate stroke of serendipity on social media, they approached me to share a little page from my diary and that entire idea fascinated me, it was then that I came to know about their distinctive page that has featured so many people around the country, and helped people share their thoughts and emotions. As a person who is constantly engaged with social media platforms and writers, I have realized that although social media have created a plethora of opportunities for us to share moments about our lives, how to get the right audience for our thoughts is still a mystery for many. And that's why I am thankful to Diary Souls for giving me and many others this amazing opportunity to share our stories and give a title to them.

The moments of enjoyment that I had while reading this book, I am sure others too will enjoy and feel inspired while going through the pages of this book (or diary). I believe every human is unique in their own way, and so are their struggles. And every individual is the calligrapher of their script. So, let us get emerged in the world of anecdotes and learn something from each of them.

I congratulate Diary Souls for their new book and hope they get successful in every step of their attempt to bring forward thousands of different stories.

-Kangkana Chakravarthy

Acknowledgements

We the team of Diary souls would like to acknowledge the trust and love of every individual, who believed in us throughout the journey, and allowed us to share their wonderful life lessons and their diaries to the world; we acknowledge the hard work of our team, in collecting stories, editing and for few fictions.

Preface

Sthuthi Dixit

This edition is all about the people who strived their best to fight their problems and took only a good part from the worst situations and left with a merry twinkle in their eyes at the end of the thunderstorm.

Everything we did till now is feasible because of the DIARY SOULS. What are these Diary souls, you all must be thinking about this? Well, Diary Souls is a constructive initiative taken to give rise to those old days' culture of writing diary entries into the present. Here everybody and anybody can jot down their whole lives roller coasters through diary writing to keep those emotions alive even after it all has already passed. It's not just an individual's diary entry but a confidential treasure house, which they can withstand and share with others.

In these busy schedules of our lives aren't we forfeited somewhere and are busy in the external world, that's the reason behind the forming of Diary Souls, to capture the memories we're about to forget. We retain our memories that are worth cherishing, and if you're busy then Diary Souls got your back. We'll write to you!

We will help you to apprehend your priceless recollections, like your wedding diary, love life, your friendship diary, your child's diary from the very moment he\she was born, we'll assist you to keep your precious moments captured together, and won't let the emotions of your moments to be lost to sight. Moments that were seized in ancient times as a part of diary writing have now become part of our history. You too can engrave your little sweet moments through Diary Souls, we're always pleased to help you.

This book encompasses part of the lives of people who stood up at junctures of difficulty. What can be greater than learning and keep getting on ahead in the distinct direction of the gust? These people shared their life stories, they conquered their fear and kept running at a time when they could barely walk, cause they had their dreams waiting for them at the end. They prevailed upon their barrier because their spirit wasn't allowing them to do otherwise. They didn't want to extinguish the burning flame in their chest, because they were not just limited to themselves but wanted to grab what they had the right to irrespective of the wounds on their body. They weren't that athletic from the start but they became one when being a strong-minded person became their top priority and their first choice because they were ready to win over the hurdles they didn't know how to deal with. A strong person can never have an easy past.

This book is created to let you all understand that you're not alone, you're not the only person who's damaged, you're not the only one walking on this highway full of obstacles, and you are wrong if you think it's not worth it. These people are just like you all, who were terrified when the problems hit them but that inner voice of theirs kept nudging them till the end. It's not like a one-night success, it's long planning and processing with a mindset of enjoying the journey. One thing I want to say about this determination to shoot at the goal.

"*"If not today, then tomorrow for sure".*"

This is the feeling that kept me and us moving forward because we believed in goodness, the essence of this life that everything that happened to me was for my good and everything that's going to happen to me will only and only be good. Everything happens to make me learn and experience so that I can be more prepared in the future. If we are not enthusiastic enough, even a small hurdle will look like a Mountain, but if we are enthusiastic enough, even a big Mountain can not stop us from getting what we want.

Diary Souls is striving to create some optimistic influence in your life. Your stories matter and we're here to take care of you and to let you know that you're not alone in this war, we're here to help you express your story. This book is going to be a hope for you all to live again, to appreciate more, to enjoy more, to laugh more, and to love more than you ever did before.

“I Might be nothing in the past,

I'm something at the present,

I’ll be everything in the future...

”

___DIARYSOULS

CHAPTER ONE

A DAY IN MY DIARY

IN A TEMPLE...

An adorable place where people visit with one motive; we ask God to bring us out of
our problems, to endow with enough money, to vouchsafe peace and happiness; Whatever
we ask we believe that God is powerful to make our wishes come true.

I just wonder how many visits temple just to thank God! Even though we all came up
with one motive, we came with different notions just like our nation, unity in diversity; some
people treat it as a holy place; Some search for fun, some visit as a nominal one, and elders
are like they are real devotees, but we all feel like we came to serve God.

Are our devotion and our steps towards the temple can be counted as wholehearted?
For instance, one young boy saw a pretty girl on temple premises; If he believes in
God and aware of devotion, how he can stare at that girl? Well, if he saw, should it be in the
temple? I just wonder here which will be more active. The soul filled with devotion or the
fleshy act of hormones? If a person sees his enemy, how he should treat him? does he has to
forgive according to the cultures of the temple? Or did he have to take his revenge according
to his heart?

Today they call it the day of God and the temple is full of rush. What about other
days? They say this day the God will have more energy than our vows will receive by him.
What about the vows on other days offered? I feel excited to know if they believe in God or
a real sense, how come they believe that God has one special day? What does this
mean? God himself says that he is present everywhere. Are we real devotees listening to
him? If yes, then why are we going to temples? The devotion should be within us. It should

not insist by others. If you believe in God, somewhat the fear of God will stop you to do bad
things. I wonder, how the world is without the word God and only with atheists. I think it
will be like... OH MY GOD!!!

CHAPTER TWO

A PROUD FARMER'S DAUGHTER

Our Inspiration

How was my Day (15/02/2020)

She was a good friend of mine for the past few months. Though we met in person sometimes and talked many times in voice and chat, I didn't ask about her family. I don't know why, suddenly I asked, "**What is your father?**"

Her answer inspired me to write this and can't stop sharing it with you...

If she says simply, "**My father is a farmer"**, It may not lead me to write this in my diary. But her answer inspired me to add a page that fills with the words... Farmer, Fields, Agriculture, Farming, Daughter-Father love, Food, Earth, etc. and I'm glad for this. She proudly replied, "Dhesaniki Annan pedathaadu (**The one who Feeds the world**)" These days, some people hesitate to say, that their family does farming. But she's not. She is proud and gratified to say that her father is a **farmer**.

I wonder why these governments don't concentrate on farming and farmers; I remember the saying, "**Once in a while, you may need a doctor but every day you need a farmer.**" I'm fortunate to have a conversation with her and know the following things are about a farmer and his greatness.

Our strength is a farmer; Farmer is giving us life to breathe fresh air, and food to live, The cotton shirt you are wearing is a farmer; He is protecting your shyness, Those flowers you gifted to your valentine is a farmer; He stands for your love, the image you see in a mirror is a Farmer; You are you because of farmer if we connect the dots, everything in this world can be connected to the great farmer

If we take care of our farmer, if we respect our farmer, if we enrich our farmer, the world goes Green and the living beings can live happily;

We need to compare the farming percentage from the olden days to now and the hospitals' percentage from past years to now. The result will shock us, There's an absolute necessity for all of us to think about this comparison and Farmer.

"*On this day, I would like to say*
THANK YOU... FARMER"

CHAPTER THREE

Manikyam

Manikyam

This is a story of Manikyam, who from his childhood grew up by
rearing goats and enjoying nature, he treated goats as his family members
and he strongly believes that **drinking goat's milk** would

be energetic &
keeps the person feeling **the warmth**.

He has 3 sons and one daughter, who said to sell the goats and take rest but as his wife who knows about his love on goats denied selling, But still, he was forced to sell & left with
half of them, Even though he has 10 acres of land he still enjoys & feels
happy in rearing the goats...

At present, the world is changing but still he
believes drinking **goat's milk is healthy**, it would enhance the
immunity power of person and no Virus can attack,
I thank him for his story and hope it will be helpful, we all know that
India's Covid -19 recovery rate is 63% and we stood at the safest
position in the battle with an invisible enemy just because of the practices of
our grandparents and like this kind of people...

CHAPTER FOUR

THAT ONE TRIP

WE

Here I am Gowtham, Medico from Andhra Pradesh, Kakinada. I
completed my graduation in Russia. Currently doing an internship in

GGH.

Aug 29, 2021: A page filled with many memories and emotions in my
Diary. As part of our internship, we were posted in a rural health center
for one month. During that time, besides our regular duties, we just
want to explore nearby beautiful places, And that is the **Maredumilli**
(forest area). It's a thrilling experience in nature; if that journey goes with friends that experience and joy will be at the next level, breathing fresh air between greens and blues is splendid.

These people are total strangers to me till before one month. As I was
graduated from another place, they are new to me; I met them on
August 1; But within a short period, we became so close... The whole one
the month was filled with laughter and learning, as happy days went like a world without a clock, the same thing happened for us; One month went just like a
day, and after this tour, my heart became heavy to realize that one-
month posting is over and I am going to miss all those memories with
them; They all became my family.

This day bus reached us to pick us up around 3 AM, By 3:15 all got on
the bus except me, It became 4:15 for me to get ready and get on the

bus; for every 10 minutes, someone comes to my room to take me; I used to say, just 10 minutes and send them, Like that... it passed one hour,(LOL) As soon as I get on the bus, everyone started clapping and whistling, It was like frustrated fun there; this incident is like... I never forget and I guess they also. (LOL)

Our journey to Maredumilli crossing the beautiful hills and having fun on the bus with these guys went so well. After that, we enjoyed ourselves a lot under waterfalls and with the beautiful sceneries around there, Photoshoots, cracking jokes, food; I was just away from the busy world on that day, in between all this fun, one of my friends tried to do an act to impress his crush and failed, Seeing it we all laughed, and it created so much fun there,(LOL). And many other memorable incidents go on with each person.

Whatever it's not easy to be with same joy while return, Some type of missing feel comes into our mind and it ruins our mood; But the memories we packed there bring us back again, I wish to thank each the person for giving such everlasting memories to my life.

Create as many memories as you can.

CHAPTER FIVE

Nrityangna

AYUSHI

Hello, World. .. This is Aayushi, born and brought up in Delhi and am a

Biotechnologist. I have my love equally spread for Dancing and Acting.

Have learned Kathak for 5 years and Belly dance for like 4

or 4.5 years.
I am right now getting training in classical singing as well!
People love my mimicking talent as well; they often give lots of love to
my Shinchan character!
I have a nuclear family of 4 people including me, Mummy, papa, and a
younger brother!
My parents have always been supportive towards my dancing or any
other talent/skill :)

The biggest challenge was and is still the society! They just keep poking
their nose in what others are doing! When I was in my college
in the second year, I introduced belly dancing, and I used to teach it to my
students! I remember people judging me out and taunting me like 'arey
in ladkiyo ka sahi hai paet dikha dikha ke ladke fasalo'
They used to body-shame me, raised questions on my character, and
many more!
But I never gave it back to them or fought with any of them, just kept on
doing what I loved to do; gradually people started understanding this
art form and started supporting me!

I remember it was my last performance in the college and before I
entered the stage, I could hear loud cheering sounds for me
-

AAYUSHI AAYUSHI AAYUSHI! And I guess that was already my winning
moment.

every faculty, the admin sir, the students, everyone appreciated my
performance personally!
And at the farewell, I was awarded as the 'Toe Twinkler- technically, the
the best dancer of college' :)

So I saw this video of Meher Malik performing on IGTV on youtube and I
was mesmerised ki yaar ye kya chiz hai !!
I also wanna do it!
How is she moving her belly so swiftly??
And those isolations man!!
So I searched more about this form, watched videos on youtube, tried
to learn through some tutorials but wanted to learn it professionally!
So one day, I watched this video of Eshan Hilal sir dancing with Meher
mam on 'tujhe dekha to' from DDLJ and I was mind blown!

I followed him everywhere and wanted to meet him anyhow!
To my luck, he conducted a workshop very near to my place, I went
there met him and took the class :)

And after that I guess khuda zyda meherbaan tha, he watched my
moves, liked them, and soon I started regular classes with him!

My learning experience with him was super fun and encouraging! He is
an awesome teacher :)

Then after that, I explored more and learned different patterns,
techniques, theories, and ideologies from international teachers!
And this journey is still on :)

"Care about only those People,

whom you think will cry,
if you die.

All these people around you won't cry."

___DIARYSOULS

CHAPTER SIX

Dear parents...I'm with you

Suma Latha

Who is Sumalatha? Sumalatha is by the blood of her parents... Right?

Yes... I am nothing without my parents, they stood for me before my
birth itself, their sacrifices, their love, and their caring towards me...
wowww... Oh, God... You are great, Thank you so much for giving
such great parents to me.

A simple girl with many dreams, But one dream that became my life are to become a
Lawyer or Civil servant, Out of these... I always think about seeing my
parents happy, they will be, Because I am there for them, for their
happiness, I am here to do anything.

I have a dream of getting into civil services, And I know the difficulty in
it I am not afraid of it, But... I believe having a substitute for everything is
good for life, So I decided to have some other dream besides being a
civil aspirant; Here comes "Vakeelsaab" into the scene, After watching
it, I got respect for Lawyers and was inspired by it, I wanted to opt
for Law; This might be crazy to hear, But yes it's the truth; Now I am
pursuing **BA LLB with IAS coaching** at Bangalore.

I am not good at my studies, Even I used to not have any interest in studies. When I get low marks for any of my exams,

Dad encourages me by saying these are just exams and these marks won't decide my future, You can perform well next time; Mom also supports me very much.

But mom always says about her childhood life, about her facings of problems and says that **one should never give up on their dreams**, No one will come to help you. At last, **you are the only one to live your life.**
One day we may leave this earth, But you have to take care of your siblings, It has to be one of your responsibilities.

In this way. .. Every story which mom said was inspired me to do hard work, She makes my mind feel refreshed; After all, I got an interest in studies and started getting good grades.
To come out of the busy world... we need to have some hobbies that kick the boredom or stress from our lives. I like to write quotes from my life experience and Shadow painting.

CHAPTER SEVEN

FREE BIRD

AKASHDEEP KAUR

A very warm regards to everyone, This is Akashdeep Kaur from

Chandigarh, teaching yoga since last year; As a child, I got bullied
and I was an introvert, so I never shared my thoughts with anyone even
if someone was hurting me. I was very sensitive and use to cry at every
little thing; My personality changed in my teenage when people
started calling me stone-hearted, emotionless, and many more...
Nobody had any hope for me especially my family because they
were worried about my future as I was not very good in academics, truly, my Childhood ambition was nothing specific but I used to love
teaching, other than this I like to read, paint, sing, and dance...

First, my life changed when I became a cabin crew soon after passing
out of High school and I was 18 at the time, I completed my graduation
alongside my job; then, when I met my husband he taught me how
to care, love, pamper and cook. I saw big changes in me; In short, he
made me feel happy, which I forgot a long time back; when I became a
cabin crew I explored new kinds of people and places. I just loved it;
Learned a lot of things about myself and got to know what makes me
feel happy...

In 2019 when I started my yoga journey, I realized that I wasn't enjoying my job anymore and I started thinking about what do I want to do in my life;
Due to responsibilities, I could not leave my job that year, and 2 years
later the situation was still the same; So, I thought I'm just scared of
tomorrow and nothing else. My husband supported me with my
the decision of quitting my job and doing what I like, I have done bungee
jumping, paragliding and I want to do many more adventurous things;
As I was not a certified Yoga teacher, I use to teach my family and
friends only, After leaving the job I went to Rishikesh for professional
training program and got my 200hrs yttc. Now I teach yoga to everyone.

CHAPTER EIGHT

MY DREAMS....TO FLY

Hey Hello...! I am Sumedha Anand, I live in many places due to postings
for my dad, As of now living in Air force station Ambala Cantt, I am now

in 10th standard. I am like a small girl, 14 years old with big dreams,
My interests lie in Dancing, acting, and participating in healthy debates;
Besides these, I had a career dream to become an officer in the Indian
Air force, My dad is an inspiration for my dream, Yes, I know having
a dream is not just enough to achieve them Unless we start working on
it, it takes us nowhere.

As I can't leave my passion and career, I need to have a plan and I am
happy that I had got a clear vision of my life; For me, managing time
between studies and interests was easy till my 9th standard, It's very
important to prioritize things; So... now I am concentrating more on my
studies as I have to get a good score in 10th. But still, I am giving 2
hours to work on my interests. I learned to manage things Because my
My second goal is to become a choreographer too; I take my career as a plan
A and dancer as plan B, Though my main aim is different from my interests, I am capable to do both;

Perhaps, it makes me more dedicative. I enjoy managing both without any stress. Whenever I feel
low I dance, It makes me feel fresh to work towards my aim, My
interests are like my stress busters and refreshers; Till stage, I have

enough confidence that I am good at both studies and dancing,
I have a good guide to me to achieve my goal, he is none other than
my dad is a great mentor to me, As of now, my plan is to just study
thoroughly... whatever I am studying... Later, I will go for a competitive exam
AFCAT to get into NDA.
Everyone will have some interests other than their current job or goal,
We just have to ensure that to give respect and time accordingly to
both aim and interests.

CHAPTER NINE

LAKSHMI

LAKSHMI

Hey there! I'm Lakshmi. Before I tell you about myself, I just want to appreciate all working women out there struggling and proving that they are not meant to just be locked up in a kitchen.

We are a lovely family of eight and I'm the younger one in the house, which means I get a lot of solicitude. But I'm that kind of girl who wants to lead my life independently, NO MATTER WHAT. That nature made me take small risks to make big changes in my life. When I completed my intermediate, I joined an organization as a part-time employee, my basic pay was around eight thousand, and also carried on with my education. I work all day and pull on all night for studies. Believe it or not, I hardly slept because I felt and I still feel the time is a very valuable asset and I wish I had more.

Every middle-class parent is concerned about his/her little girl's future. So did mine and compelled me not to work. They were worried not because I'm a girl, because of working late hours. It's for the reason that, what might society and relatives think of me. My dad didn't know if his baby girl could defend those mean words and face the hurdles.

As the time passed, watching me grow, watching me beat the struggles, building each step with my dedication, My parents realized that I'm much stronger than they imagined and supported me to fly high. Now I've been working for two years now. I earn three times the salary compared to the beginning of my career and I'm able to take care of my family. I've learned many things like facing the world, people's true color, and defending myself. Now, none of my family gives a damn about society's perception of our personal life.

Meanwhile, I did what I loved the most. I want to showcase my multiple talents and decided to make some sound on social media. I've been learning Carnatic Music for two years and Kuchipudi during my school days and I'm passionate about acting. So, I started making reels and singing on my Instagram. People express admiration for my skill, so did my family. I'm also getting scripts for short films. These skills make me feel alive, stress-free.

I'll plan every day to work on them and also would like to opt them as a career.

Further, I would like to pursue an MBA and help my dad in business. All I want is to walk through multiple paths which I love and reach a milestone, wear a hat of success, and gift happy tears to my family for their love and support and keeping faith in me."

CHAPTER TEN

The day I learnt to smile

RESHMITHA SIVANI

Hai.. . I'm Reshmitha Sivani from Vishakapatnam. I'm a Pharm.D student and Robinhood Army volunteer. I'm happy to share my experience with Diarysouls.

Here is the story of how an eight-year-old, changed my perspective towards life.

When you visit an orphanage for the first time, you would expect a bit of despair. But, kids in any orphanage are warm, active, and smart.

My story started, when I met Bhavani, an eight-year-old. She had big round eyes. I gave her a banana and she smiled at me saying "THANKS AKKA". She had the brightest smile and it was straight from the heart, it's contagious and I smiled back. Not the regular one, the brightest smile.

I cannot fathom the sense of satisfaction I got after that 20 minutes conversation.

I cannot put a price on the time I spent at the orphanage. It's been a year and every Sunday, I get to learn new things be it kids or robins, It works as a DETOUR for me.

That one smile had a ripple effect on my life.

Every minute is an opportunity to be helpful, and it doesn't need a huge investment; just an honest thought could start massive change.

When I got an opportunity to write my first paper at a medico-legal conference at GITAM, I chose to write about adoption under the category of assisted reproductive technology.

There are more orphans in the world than the couples who could afford surrogacy." Adoption is an ethical and most effective solution to stop wombs from being rented. Commercial or altruistic surrogacy affects many lives in the long run whereas adoption can give new life to a disowned child.

It was a bold decision. But I was pretty confident because I knew "If anyone has a choice to pick between safest and most effective ART and Bhavani's smile. They would pick that priceless smile. "

"Girls own the word beauty...

Never try to own it by cheating...

They turn more gorgeous when they desire to earn you...

so...

Don't try to steal them, earn them"

CHAPTER ELEVEN

PRATHIKSAA

Prathiksaa

Hi ,this is Prathiksaa from Tamilnadu ..
?I started my journey of life in the early '20s and ever since I have been up against barriers and met many different types of characters. All with their gain is put first without a thought for others. Wow now this stage of my life that

made me who I am today, it had the most life-changing experiences up to this date.

?Fortunately, my thirst for knowledge did not come to an end when I was at school. I was passionate about maths and science. This passion helped me gain profound knowledge in these areas, and I was admitted to the college of my dreams. Today, I am a student at an engineering college and I feel very happy about it. I am certain that my degree will become my ticket to a better tomorrow. I study hard and devote my free time to reading scholarly reviews and watching interviews with recognized specialists in the field, of course, I understand that life is not just a bed of roses, and challenges and hardships are an integral element of life.

?Everyone will agree that hard work never fails, the day I felt very prouder was two weeks ago..the day when my first achievement came true. yes, I was very happy to hear that. I'm the first person who completed salesforce out of 3000+ students all over India. I was interviewed by an industrial person. I felt very happy to hear heartful wishes from my friends and professors. I hope in the future, my achievements will help needy people to satisfy their needs. And thanks diarysouls for asking my story... This made me emotional...

?And this helped me a lot to recollect my memories...

CHAPTER TWELVE

KARTHIK.KARTHIKA

Hey guys... Karthi Nambiar here from Kerala, I used to work in a finance company here in
Oman; I like acting, makeovers adapting to new looks and singing also... When you find a path
to your passion, why go for a 9- 5 job? Yes, I did the same I quit the job after I came to know
that I can excel in acting and makeovers.

Tiktok may not be present in India now but it's **still in my heart**, It helped to find my inner talent that is acting and makeovers, When I used to watch the makeup artists, actors, and all those stuff, I got interested in them. Your mind will give a sign that this is hidden in you and it will ask you to bring it up. I am glad that I tried on them and got enough confidence that I can give my best, From then I started exploring myself in this field.

And I guess I am doing fine now, When I tried lady getup for first it was fun and felt like
something new, I did make up for myself; I am not good at makeup stuff. I was afraid to try, lol...
My father was shocked and laughing like hell, He said the acting was good but the getup was not
good. It was the first time I tried. mom hesitantly gave support because she wanted to see his
son's marriage with a girl and keep her sarees in her wardrobe itself. lol... My sister is my true fan
always, She always encourages and gives suggestions on jewelry and makeup kits, My other
family members appreciated my efforts, and those who don't have Insta ID they created even to
watch my reels. I got comments about what you are guessing? Yes, It's like...Are you gay?
Generally, I don't reply to those comments. Once I comment... Okay fine! to one guy. The moral
here is to take don't argue with brainless people. Some comments are necessary to bring out the
best version in us. When I got the first call from the Tamil director for the web series, I was
flying with joy. Later on, also I got a few opportunities to act in Malayalam, Telugu, and Tamil for
short films and web series. I am planning to commit those.

But this pandemic is not letting to
commit all. Soon you will see me on small screens and I wish I will hit the big screen as well.

CHAPTER THIRTEEN

NEVER STOP GROWING

Hi everyone, I am Priyanka from Tamilnadu, India.

I am a simple girl with thousands of dreams, I love to learn and explore
myself...

Apart from my journey,

I'm a state chess player, And I used to be quite studious in my childhood, I
was selected as a Young scientist by the Tamilnadu Government, And
completed my SSLC with 98% and HSC with 90%; I used to have a lot of
friends and my parents gave me all freedom to be independent, I
started my major as a chemist student in a reputed women's college; I
fed up with my routine, But I was surrounded with love, affection; To be honest, it was the best moment of my life.

But...Gods plan is always better than ours;

With God's grace, I got my medical seat in a college at

Kanyakumari
under merit, I was super excited my parents asked me, "Dear, can you
stay in a hostel for 4 &1/2 years?" And I nodded my head with tons of
happiness; Because I love to learn and explore, and it is a great
opportunity for me too, I packed all my things and got a new Android
phone, Once I entered the hostel, I was stuck with the hostel rules;
There, No mobile phones are allowed, no outings, and most importantly naturopathist, we are not supposed to eat Non-vegetarian foods.

At first, somehow I managed to do my daily regimen, As the days pass I started
receiving hatred ness from the people I love, fate is cruel to everyone
and I am not an exception; Slowly I started suffering mentally and
physically, I started to practice solitude; I distracted myself by reading
books and doing handcrafts, I spend my 24 hours in a useful way; I
practiced yoga and meditation daily during this journey I have some
good souls to lean my shoulder on; Slowly the darkness faded.

And the quarantine gives me the break; which I needed most in my life, I
spend time with my family;
The year 2020 changed my life completely, I started

perceiving things
differently, I saw so many people are suffering physically, mentally, and
financially; I just want to help them, As a Naturopathy and Yoga doctor, I
wish everyone would lead a healthy and happy life; When I think about
in this pandemic situation, **I planned to start a blog.**

With my personal experience and knowledge, I started posting healthy
updates And I healed so many people with my posts;
Believe me, I saw the best version of myself, the painful
path makes lots of wonders to my life,
I hope I am on the right path to chase my dreams, **several milestones are on my way** to
achieve.

Life is all about struggles and success; For a seed to grow, it needs
sunshine, water, and soil; So, forget the worries and keep moving. You
become what you think, Believe in yourself, and explore yourself. Learn
from your mistakes and be positive.

Live every moment and Never stop growing

CHAPTER FOURTEEN

BUSHRA'S DIARY

BUSHRA AMEER

This is Bushra Ameer from Sri Lanka, I'm an LLB degree holder by
the university of London, I thought everything is going well; You know what life is
very crazy;
My father had passed away 8 years ago, My mother doing a

small
business supplying stitched clothes to a shop, I started to experience changes in my health.

I wish no one should have a story like mine, I'm a kidney patient who is
waiting for a kidney transplant; I have one brother, a private employee,
He is the first person who came forward to donate a kidney, but unfortunately
it didn't match to me, I have no other option than to buy outside, I have seen
many ups and downs in my 28 years of life. Seeing my condition, the doctor
wrote Angiogram test (test related to the heart), The result showed four
blocks in my heart; now I have to go bypass as well, now the expense
around me is more than 50 lakhs, these days I'm thinking about that
money for operations; while having no money in hand for doctor
consultation at least, I started fundraising till now we got 10 lakhs
through my friends and loved ones; Still to get much much more for me
to stand on this earth; I believe in God and he will help me for sure.

My health is deteriorating day by day, Sometimes I feel like the end is
coming soon to my life before something happens to me feeling like to
see the beauty of the world by exploring it, but I never

wanted to be
demotivate and feel sad and depressed; I have to be strong for my mother
and for the people who love me and help me.

> "*If we believe in ourselves and our good deeds,*
> *we can change any situation;*
> *I believe that and so I accepted these downs with me.*"

In this life, I couldn't save a lot of money but I got some awesome people
around me... One week back, my friends took me on a trip to Ella which is
a beautiful travel destination in Srilanka to make me cheer up...Those
two days are the best days of my life to forget all my problems and
laughed my heart out though still, my stomach started to pain.

CHAPTER FIFTEEN

PALAK CHHABRA DIARY

You are the CEO of your Life (Hire, Fire And Promote Accordingly)

This is Palak Chhabra from Rajasthan, I am currently working as a researcher, I write on international affairs, The one page that I wish to share in Diarysouls is... This incident is of my college days in Pune, when we all were gearing up for our internships, I wanted to get into the Ministry of External Affairs anyhow... But, my director for some reason never used to like me, she called me in her office and said, "See Palak, I know everyone's standards over here" This line pinched me to the core, that very day I decided to get the internship at my own cost; All my batch mates had already completed their internships and I had not even started mine, I got an ultimatum from college that it is not their lookout anymore, then the day came when I got an email of my selection at the Ministry, I jumped in joy; My director came to know about it but she didn't react, She asked everyone about their internship experiences except me, for obvious reasons... But that day I won! I did.

You know you are lucky if you come across people who say you can't do it; And when you finally, prove them wrong, that feeling is out of the world.

"I might be nothing to you
But, I am something to myself.

I realized something is better than nothing.
So, I chose to be something"

____DIARYSOULS

CHAPTER SIXTEEN

MY 21ST BIRTHDAY BLITZ

SNEHAL

When you get the wishes from your loved ones on your birthday, it
gives you a lot of joy and happiness. If someone asks me for

the best wish I got on my birthday, how can I differentiate between all the best wishes?

Hey all... This is Snehal from Maharashtra. Here I am sharing the birthday page from my Diary. It was my birthday on 26-06-2021. I thought that this year no one will come to celebrate my birthday. But In any case, my best friend will be there with me. I guessed that simply I will be cutting a cake at home with my family and spending time with my bestie. Perhaps, that will be more for anyone in this pandemic situation.

lol...

But to my surprise, a few of my friends joined along with my bestie. It made me feel so special. I am like a person who always likes to live a private life. I am not very sociable. I just focus on my life and work. Besides me being like this also, they came and celebrated my birthday. I realized that this is true friendship. You may not be in regular communication with your friends. It doesn't mean that relation or the bond we had is gone. That's still there. I am glad to have friends like them.

Birthday is the day when strangers also make you feel good just by wishing. Birthday is always special for me no matter what's going on in my life and what happened in the whole year.

This time so many of my friends and family members felt upset because I slept early at night. They rang my phone many times to wish me. My best friend calls me before 5 minutes to midnight and continues to have a call with me till the date shifts. So that she can be the only one to wish me first. She is a great person indeed. She always tries to make me feel special as like no one is there to do anything for me special other than her.

Everyone on their birthday expects wishes from a few people. When you get all those special wishes from special persons, the day would be completed. I am happy that my birthday was completed with those special wishes.

"***HAPPY BIRTHDAY TO ME....!!!!***"

CHAPTER SEVENTEEN

ONE SNAKE...THREE HOURS

A snake in a hole...around that hole many people...no-one is dared to kill it. I am too afraid of snakes. The fear among all people is the same that if it misses, it may keep a grudge and
follows them. Some young boys have dared to distract it. But their
well-wishers don't want them to do it. Only two or three people in
my street dare to kill the snakes. Even my dad is afraid of snakes.
See here.., The main motive of everyone around it is finishing its
life only whether it is poisonous or not poisonous but not letting it
out from that remote place to its safe place. Even am also the
same in that thought. What a devotion mind for us! We

pray to
snakes only in temples as in rocks. We kill them when they are
with life. As I am educated I can understand that one should not
believe in superstitions about snakes. But the other side, I cannot
remember them in a live situation. I have to believe in the old
systems because all the people around me are who follow them.
At least if I try to let them know about what I know, it won't work
out. In real I won't take that step because, though am educated
some worry will stop me. The worry is that it may cause harm to
anyone.
Finally, after a long time, the snake was killed by one of those two
dared persons.

Moral: It's very hard to change the Indians' psychology.

CHAPTER EIGHTEEN

UNEMPLOYED

There's a man called "**Unemployed**"
Once he started his journey to make friends with his dream friend
"**Employment**"
In starting of his journey, He faced many persons, "**Rejections**"
But he was never demotivated. Because he is carrying "**Confidence**" in his
bag and "**Trust**" in his heart.
One of his friends suggested meeting " **Skill**" and "**Learn**". He told him
that they will take him to "**Employment**".

He took the Right turn and started exploring for "**Skill**" and "**Learn**".
Finally, he met them. He started to move with them closely and know
about them everything. He invested his time to spend with them
mostly. "**Learn**" taught him everything. He gained all the knowledge
about them. He realized how to search and meet "**Employment**" in

"Jobs" World.

Now he packed his bag again and started his journey.

Let's go deeper into his story on the next part.

CHAPTER NINETEEN

RAMAKRISHNA'S STORY

RAMA KRISHNA

I'm Ramakrishna (I don't know who kept this name to me, I used to be
called like that...)
I don't know my parent's face, I don't know who gave birth

to me, I was
grown up in an Ashram in Karnataka;
After that I was taken by somebody to work, In return, I used to get
abused, I ran from there and do small works here and there; I don't want to create any relations there's no one to take
care of me, and to get acquainted with me; I used to think of only work
and earn enough for food.

Years passed on and my strength got decreased, I never want to beg;
I know It's not a respectable way, As I can walk around I used to earn some
amount using the weighing machine in the markets.

Now I can't move here and there around markets, I find peace under
the trees, I simply sit under the tree and think about God. For
the first three days, when I was here under this tree I didn't receive any
food, Later some people recognized me and start offering some food; By
God's grace from that day through someone, I get food; which I don't want to
waste, Some nights I don't get any; I store some which I got morning
times and eat it. If I get excess food for the day, I give that food to
someone like me nearby the temple.

One policeman said... Don't uncover your mask, Without asking

some people are giving me food, For their sake, I don't want to take out
my mask.

These dogs are my friends... I can understand their appetite; We eat
together.

I don't want to comment anything on life and Money, I just find peace
closing my eyes and thinking about God.

But, one thing to say;

> "***Hunger, pain, and cold are the same for every living being;***
> ***so, be kind to all.***"

God bless you all.

CHAPTER TWENTY

GATEWAY TO PEACE

That day was SILENT'S birthday. It decided to give a party and invited all
fellows.
The SORRY said it can't attend the party.
MR.ATTITUDE, ANGRY, THE RESPECT and all other his friends
attended the party. HUNGER came at the dinner time. During the
dinner, ATTITUDE started to behave intensely with inheritance.
It spoiled the entire party's mood. The SILENT accompanied CALM
and stared helplessly. ANGRY got angrier seeing his behavior. The
RESPECT feeling like she lost all respect. STUPID tried to stop him. Then
the ARGUMENT enters. The PATIENCE is almost over raged.
The HELP was on the way to the party. SILENT and TENSION asked the

THINK, 'How to stop this?'
Then the THINK said, everything will set now. See, SMILE is coming.

SMILE entered the party room and faced the ATTITUDE and smiled.
Sooner, the PEACE stepped in there along with her friend HAPPY. The
SATISFY witnessed the FUN, ENJOY dancing and singing with all the
Party members.

GRATITUDE saying thanks to their fellows left to home. Finally, the
the party ended happily with CRAZINESS and Jokes.

> "*"If the ATTITUDE and SMILE meet... Then PEACE enters."*"

"Never let your fears

bury your dreams."

CHAPTER TWENTY-ONE

BEYOND WHAT YOU SEE...

HARSHITH SRIVASTHSAV

I am Harshit from Rajahmundry, AP... here's my story beyond what you
see me actually;
I am a multi-talented person, I sing, I play, I draw, I write, I

do a lot of
others things, though many people know about what talents I have,
only a few people know that I have been able to excel in them equally.
Say, for instance, no one knows that I sing, even if they do, they don't
know how well I do...
Coming to my life, I have put myself into various things like acting,
directing, scriptwriting, poetry, book writing, and a lot more, But out of
all only art came out to the public as it was able to do something
permanent Rest of them is more experiential; That doesn't mean I didn't
face challenges in the field of art.

I was encouraged by a lot of people in the field of art but also
discouraged by many, They used to say - Art doesn't feed you..!
I used to be mocked, a lot of times. But the same people used to come
for a favor when it's their need.

I have always been looked like a weird guy with behavior, talents,
lifestyle and interests which are quite different from others...
But after a few years of rigorous determination, I've put into the art and
after becoming a moderately well-known person, the word

"Weird"
suddenly changed to something called "Unique".

I have been doing a lot of good deeds with my art, like donations and
adoptions. For those who said my art doesn't feed me - it is feeding tens
of hungry stomachs.

As with academics, I strived to get into Architecture and I received very
discouraging comments like "architecture cannot be done by a mere
artist".

But I cracked the entrance exams by myself, with basic training.
Towards the end and I'm topping in my Department now. I'm also
excelling with my freelance works.

In the end, what I say is Architecture made me into a knowledgeable
person and art tuned me to become a better version of my true self. It is
only my strength and determination that inspired me to face any
situation in life... Now that I have confidence about facing any situation
in life, I always say - I'm high on life.

**The experience it gives is more
wonderful and permanent than what any other thing can give.**

CHAPTER TWENTY-TWO

The endured warrior

Lishamol K D

Hey World! This is Lishamol K D from Kottayam, Kerala; I am a nursing student, It's fact and fate, I wished to be a doctor, But I am a nursing professional now; After all, I am very happy and proud to be a nurse as I can give care and service to people, It's a kind of doctor Right? lol

Other than this. .. I was always fascinated to be a fashion model and grow with fame as Lisha K D. I always feel to create my style without copying others for fashion and trends; But, I used to be shy and sad about my dark skin. It's all because of the journey I had with societal racialism towards dusky tone. Unfortunately, I lost some of my friends due to this critical racism.

I was put back in some events during schooling and outside as well; they used to call me many nicknames like Black girl, dark girl, dark skinner, and many more like that. I was rejected for many photoshoots because of my dark skin;

> "*I was depressed, broken, and upset with my skin tone.*"

But now, I am very happy that it was all in past, I passed it successfully And now I feel to be blacker than I am, Happy to bear this skin tone as the trends are going with dark skin currently; It happened

to see those
trends, I gained confidence. Slowly I am on a way to photoshoots as well.

I overcame all the dark past and came out of all the bad/ negative
comments. Now I am not hearing them at all; In fact, People started to
praise my beauty and smile. I reached the level where I can take any
comments from my family itself; So now negative comments on my skin
tone or costumes from the public don't matter to me at all.

The only place where I enjoyed being myself is my home with my parents
and siblings, I am proud to have them always; They always support and
encourage me with my acts.

***I am on a way to go through my career goal as well as my professional
goal.***

> "
>
> *"I will be sharing my story like how I am getting opportunities, and how I
> am taking steps and how I am overcoming the difficulties and many
> more."* "

CHAPTER TWENTY-THREE

DIVYA

DIVYA

Hai... Namaste!
I'm Divya from Anantapur . I'm an Enthusiastic learner and loves exploring new skills. Happy to share my learning

experience with @diarysouls

If you open my recent pages in my diary during this lockdown, you will read all my learning experiences.

I aim to get a placement in a good MNC company. I realized sitting idle and thinking about the dream can't make us reach near to our dream. There's a vast difference between learning the skills to implementing the skills that we have learned practically. My experience led me to know the difference.

This lockdown taught me many things. Out of many, it gave me much learning experience. I fell more in love with learning the skills and implementing them. I enjoy it in abundance.

When we were in schools and colleges, we will be having some set of rules, instructions, orders framed by others and we have teachers, mentors/guides to lead us and make us learn. There we may find Joy or maybe no to learn. But believe me, if you start learning yourself being a teacher to yourself, the more joy you can find and more knowledge you gain. You will feel splendid to learn.

At the start, you may feel difficult to learn but if you continue to learn continuously you will experience interest and love towards learning.

I'm learning software courses at udemy. .. We spend money going to a theatre... Skip one movie and invest that money and purchase a course in udemy/Coursera/ Edx. Sometimes you can find free courses and at very low cost as below as 500rs on different platforms. Try to explore them.

> “" *Implementing the skill we are learning in practice is important* "”

Hope sure through learning and implementing the skills in real life will make my life happy by achieving my dreams. I was frustrated to read " we know that " in books in my academics without any practical knowledge. And I wish this New Education Policy creates change and enhances the skills of students.
Thank you.

CHAPTER TWENTY-FOUR

TWIN YOGINIS

Hriday And Manas

Namaste, Dear world!
I am Manasmaitri along with my twin Hridaymaitri
On this rosy International Yoga Day, we wish you to have a healthy and soulful life; adding a spoon of encouragement with our story, we are too glad to serve the zest of our TWIN YOGA.

After 9 months together we left each other for 5min to see this world, we may born to enlighten yoga in the newest way with new motives, and we may vary when it comes to coordination and thoughts which can be rectified, Yoga has many teachers many motives which and who are worth lionize, Our lane of Yoga was known as TWIN YOGA, we named it on our twinship. Before covid, I thought of creating a Yoga page and discussed it with my sister about the idea. She was excited and said, " why not? We can start together and name it TWIN YOGINIS. There all started the idea of TWIN YOGINIS. In the initial days..., We were mostly inspired by the Bihar School of Yoga. We never went to classes there. We just followed their learnings and teachings on different platforms. It was closed during all the covid times and, we do not have any intention to go to that Ashram for classes. It remained an inspiration and motivation for us from then to till. Covid became a bane it is also a boon in several stages. We were included in them. We utilized that time in the house to gain more knowledge in Yoga and do better in partner Yoga

In amidst journey, we found out that partner yoga is practiced in other countries, we also discovered we are the first twins to come forward to preach yoga together, many industries witnessed the success of twins in various fields now, and even yoga started witnessing the grace of twinship.

As like old saying "Practice makes a man perfect" every day we practice single/normal yoga, and for content and shoot we prefer partner yoga, "Two is better than one" as two develop the understanding abilities in each other, it helped us to understand each other's Trust and body language, we communicate through our bodies, which is a kind of intellectual way of connecting each other's spirits, we find some sort of joy while doing yoga, as from beginning we learned and changed a lot, we got each other's back in a while.

Yoga is not about bending and stretching's, it's about a healthy lifestyle, no need for advanced yoga but basic stretches in daily patterns help for physical health, even there's a kind of psychological enlightening in yoga, where sitting quietly in the Dhyana position helps to refresh. So many myths wrapped in yoga; they say yoga is a boring exercising practice, but in reality, it is just a myth. To know the truth one must start doing basic yoga.

we are looking forward to wiping out myths that people are having and encouraging people to practice them daily.

We Twin Yoginis started to build our bond, trust each other and do what makes us happy.

We are promoting partner yoga to everyone. Anyone working on a relationship, creating a new one, or even struggling to mend a relationship, can work on it or it can be just a fun activity too to challenge yourself. Giving up is easy and working on something to improve takes time, effort, and consistency.

But why yoga when everyone finds it boring. Yoga is an all-rounder from working on strength to flexibility or even balancing hormones. Yoga is for all ages, body types, occupations, or locations, customizable to your needs. Yoga is the answer for body, mind, and soul.

Through consistency and determination, we are making yoga part of our lives, investing our efforts and time to inspire and connect.

We are also keeping social media close to reality as much as possible. Be yourself, everyone else is already taken.

We twins will make you move

How Yoga worked in our lives:

I Manasmaitri, faced a lot of comparison in this rival world, as we know growing up is not that easy, I faced more psychological suppression and some mental assaults in my daily life, and I faced so many inner battles which led me to self-doubt and kind of trauma, I started doing yoga to reduce my stress, especially for my mental health and it even helped me with my physical health, after I started yoga, I saw changes in my temper and in my way of thinking.

Hridaymaitri:

In my fifth standard.., an ear infection started slowly later when I entered college, My left ear started bleeding, Then we consulted a doctor and got a suggestion for surgery but, I had gone through three surgeries in four years; So I had to take bed rest, you know what it feels like to stay in bed for sports kinda person, It's kinda physical and mental torture, After these surgeries for two years, I faced other issues as well; like irregular periods, Weight gain, Knee pains, and imbalances; I was not able to concentrate on my fitness. But this idea of creating a Yoga page and continuous practice on yoga helped me a lot to come back with my fitness and it helped me a lot with my ear infection as well...From then I was able to focus on well-being

CHAPTER TWENTY-FIVE

GIVE TIME TO THE THINGS YOU LOVE

Give time to the things You Love

Hai All. .. I am Shivani from Gujarat. Here my story goes.

I've loved dancing since I was a little kid. I've always enjoyed moving to music and expressing lyrics through it. So it is difficult to point out an exact moment where I fell in love with it.

I understood the significance of dance in my life when I started working a full-time job in Delhi. I would seek solace in dance. It became my way to unwind, to let go of all the work stress. Dance took a more meditative form during the pandemic because it helped me stay centred and grounded.

It was during the pandemic that I started posting videos on my Instagram account. I've always been inspired by Madhuri Dixit, Banjara Girls led by Meher Malik and off lately my belly dance teacher Aakriti Gandhi. The rain and sea are also an inspiration sometimes. I think dance has become a habit. So some days, I don't need to motivate myself.

It's been a huge challenge to believe in my dancing especially because there are so many dancers on social media. I do have thoughts about not being good enough, not being trained enough or being versatile.

I had started posting my videos on my personal account, which received a lot of positive comments and encouraged me to believe in my dance and moreover the ability to make the audience smile through it. I rarely think of not being good enough because somewhere, I've found my little brand of dancing and I'm learning dance at the same time to keep enhancing my skills.

I also find it challenging to keep creating choreographies back to back without taking breaks. Staying relevant on Instagram is a tedious task. I usually take long breaks at times as I'm unable to create something. Those days I dance for myself in front of the mirror or practice moves I've already learnt. It usually helps to get back to creating choreography.

The rest of my story will be on the next pages of my Diary,

"Shivani

(Give time to the things You Love)"

Thank you.

←←→→←_←

We Preserve Your Memories

Diary Souls is our little trail to preserve the world's blissful moments and to bring shape for your memories, that have been treasured deep in your hearts

In this digital era, people focus on temporary pleasures and livelihood instead of building palaces and being mummified in monuments; We thought of being happy in many ways and ended up getting two eye-catching photographs and 150 not considered, when we turn back to look at the memory the only thing we can glance is those two photographs and temporary videography which reminds the struggle of earning those, but where do your moments go?

We are getting involved in capturing our moments instead of making memories, DiarySouls help you to preserve your memories, Just go and live the moment and remember it, Our team is all yours, we'll hear and will live with you to record every moment of you and produce it as a modern diary without any struggle in your days.

Live and Love; Spit and Get
Memories in your hand

9 798887 497280

Printed by Libri Plureos GmbH in Hamburg, Germany